If Your Tears were Human

A Collection of Poetry for Animals in Agriculture

SECOND EDITION

WHO chains YOU PUBLISHING

HEATHER LEUGHMYER

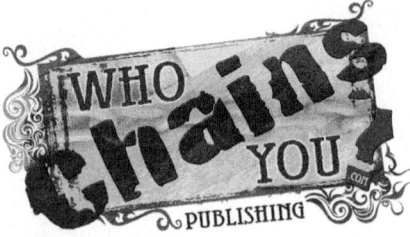

Published by Who Chains You Publishing
P.O. Box 581
Amissville, VA 20106

www.WhoChainsYou.com

Written by Heather Leughmyer
Photography by Vanessa Sarges
Photo of girl and her goat by Heather Leughmyer

ISBN-13: 978-1-946044-65-5

Printed in the United States of America

Second Edition

This collection of poetry is lovingly dedicated to

THE BILLIONS OF ANIMALS WHO SUFFER AND DIE AT THE HANDS OF

HUMANS TO BECOME "FOOD"; AND TO ALL THE COMPASSIONATE AND

COURAGEOUS INDIVIDUALS WHO FIGHT FOR THEM EVERY SINGLE DAY.

"Think occasionally of the suffering of which you spare yourself the sight."

—ALBERT SCHWEITZER

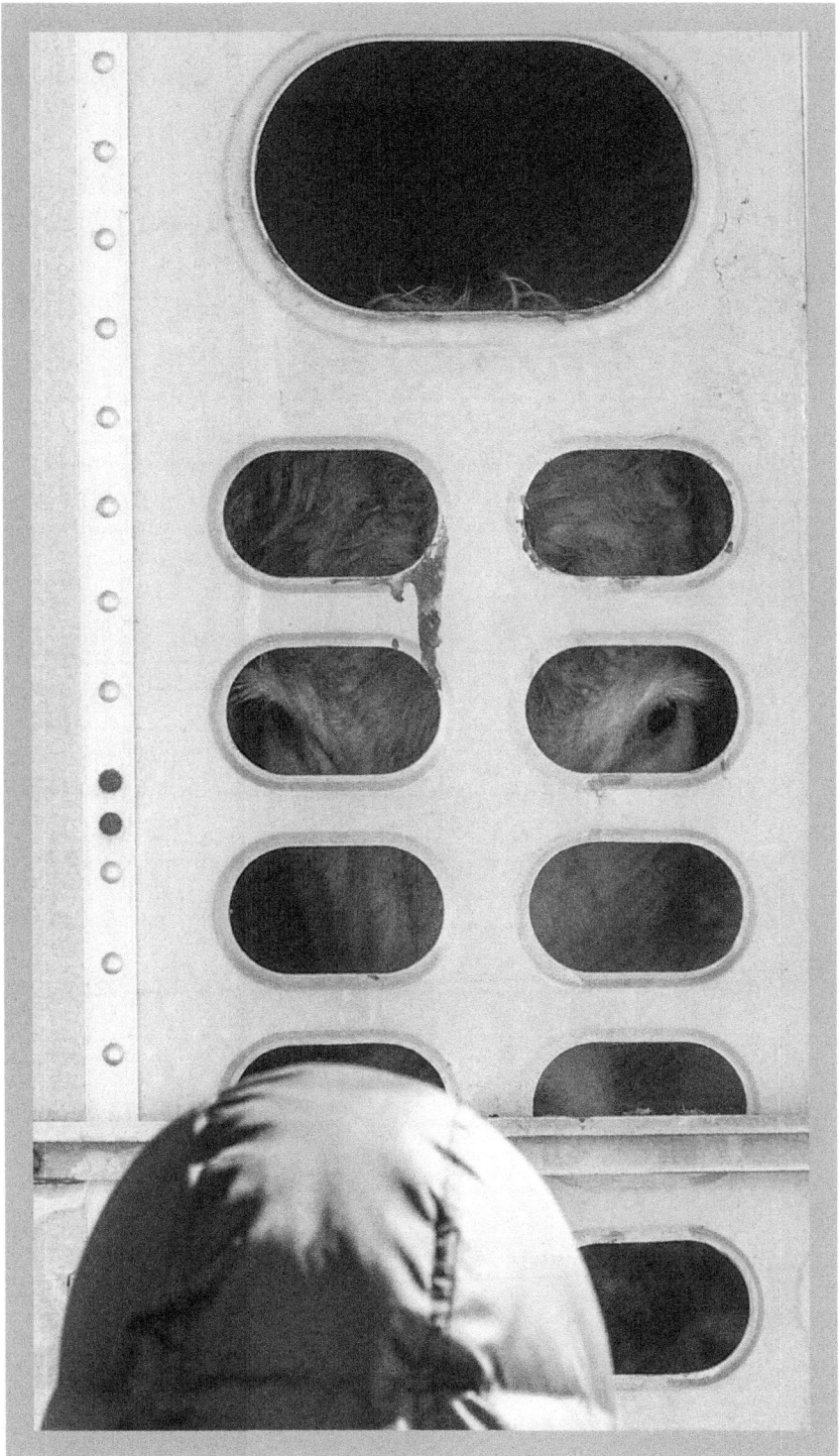

Table of Contents

Introduction

Each year, billions of land animals are raised and killed for their meat, eggs, and milk. To the agricultural industry, they are not living, feeling beings. They are commodities; they are dollar signs. But to a growing number of people from all walks of life, these precious souls are not just production units to be owned and exploited. They have purpose beyond our palates. They are unique individuals who experience pleasure and pain. They are companions, they are teachers, and they bring beauty and diversity to the planet we all share.

Today, many people are choosing not to participate in the violence inherent in this vile industry. They are banding together and becoming a voice for these oppressed innocents. They are forming animal "Save" groups in which they bear witness to animals on their way to slaughter in order to give them some small semblance of dignity before they die. These people see them as more than just the numbers that they have been branded or tattooed with, and through photographs, they document the abysmal conditions and give each animal a face in order to educate others about their plight.

Many others are discovering the vast advantages of a plant-based diet that excludes all animal flesh and byproducts. This choice not only greatly decreases animal suffering; it also shrinks our environmental footprint and is beneficial to human health. Vegan alternatives to animal products are now readily available at mainstream grocery stores and restaurants, and vegan cookbooks and recipes are plentiful. Transitioning to a vegan lifestyle is now easier than ever before.

Farmed animal sanctuaries are popping up all over the world. These picturesque farms offer a safe, peaceful haven for a few lucky individuals who, for various reasons, received a reprieve from the horrors of animal agricultural. Many of them arrive frightened, ill or injured, but with a little time and a lot of compassion, they learn to trust again and their personalities blossom. In these places, animals who had never before known human kindness are given a second chance at life.

I hope to encourage and empower others to live a more compassionate existence. The poems included in this book were inspired by animals, people and events I have encountered at some point in my animal activism. Although I have been deeply disturbed by the magnitude of human cruelty toward these innocent beings, I have been touched just as deeply by the people who are brave enough to protest these injustices and who work relentlessly to make this world a less brutal place. These are my heroes; the rebels, the bunny-huggers, those with the largest hearts and the softest souls. Never give up.

—*Heather Leughmyer*

My Eyes

There are times it seems

My eyes are never dry

Every minute, every single day

Many thousands die.

For a pork chop, for a burger

Though innocent, they perish

While I mourn for beauty lost

A beauty so few cherish.

If I just closed my eyes

Life could be so good

But the darkness wouldn't hide the truth now

Even if I could.

The truth is that compassion

Could end callousness and greed

But thousands more have just lost their lives

This moment as you read.

My eyes are far from perfect

But I will not go blind

By letting my heart harden

Or by narrowing my mind.

There is a price for seeing

Life can never be the same

But to me it's not a choice

And to them, it's not a game.

So once again I'll wipe away

The tears that I have cried

And open others to the truth

For the billions that have died.

Broken

❧

Cages encompass both body and mind

Searching for freedom that they'll never find

Crated like cargo and shipped just like slaves

Money is murder, and stomachs, their graves.

There are those who are broken, whose gentle hearts bleed

Feeling helpless and hopeless in the face of pure greed

Sensing their suffering, bearing their pain

Perpetual sadness for corporate gain.

If others could see through compassionate eyes

The horror, the hurting, the desperate cries

If they could experience this continuous ache

If only their hearts could crumble and break.

If the world could embrace every breath, every being

Not just shallowly looking, but authentically seeing

Their beauty, their purpose, their desire to live

Instead of taking and wasting, they wanted to give.

Cages would be vacant, void of despair

A huge weight would be lifted off those hearts that care

The broken would heal, the innocents freed

And kindness prevail over violence and greed.

Bearing Witness

❧

Anonymous at birth

Anonymous at death

You're a piece, a part, a unit

A number with a breath.

A unique personality

With one common name

And tangible feelings

No two the same.

Few will ever meet you

Or mourn your tragic end

You never had an ally

You never had a friend.

Through portholes in the metal

Our somber eyes unite

We promise you through silent tears

We won't give up our fight.

We try our best to comfort you

Your dignity embraced

Through photographs we're changing hearts

With each angelic face.

To us you weren't an object

And although your soul's departed

We refuse to let compassion die

The ripple's only started.

Sad Crops

These crops are planted in sunless rows

Where no rain drops, and no wind blows

Where ammonia chokes with every breath

The air is thick with dust and death.

These crops are grown in secret spaces

Fields of steel line hidden places

Landscapes marred with lagoons of red

Deep and sticky, stagnant dread.

At harvest time these crops are ripped

Hung on hooks, sliced and shipped

To the freezer case at your local store

Politely packaged to mask the gore.

Her Secret

❧

In a crowded cage she sits

Ammonia chokes the air

Aside from all the feces

The wire floor is bare.

Not a strand of straw for comfort

To build a cozy nest

She lays egg after egg after egg after egg

And never gets to rest.

Her skin exposed and bleeding

Where feathers should have been

She's a shell of what she used to be

This hopeless little hen.

Never has she stretched her wings

Or scratched her feet in dirt

She's known this life forever

Deprivation, darkness, hurt.

To them she's just a "unit"

Her job is to produce

When she no longer can

She'll no longer be of use.

All she's ever known

Is her tiny metal hell

Every day enduring

The boredom, pain, the smell.

Her eggs will soon be omelets

Be deviled and be dyed

While happy cartoon hens

Keep her secret locked inside.

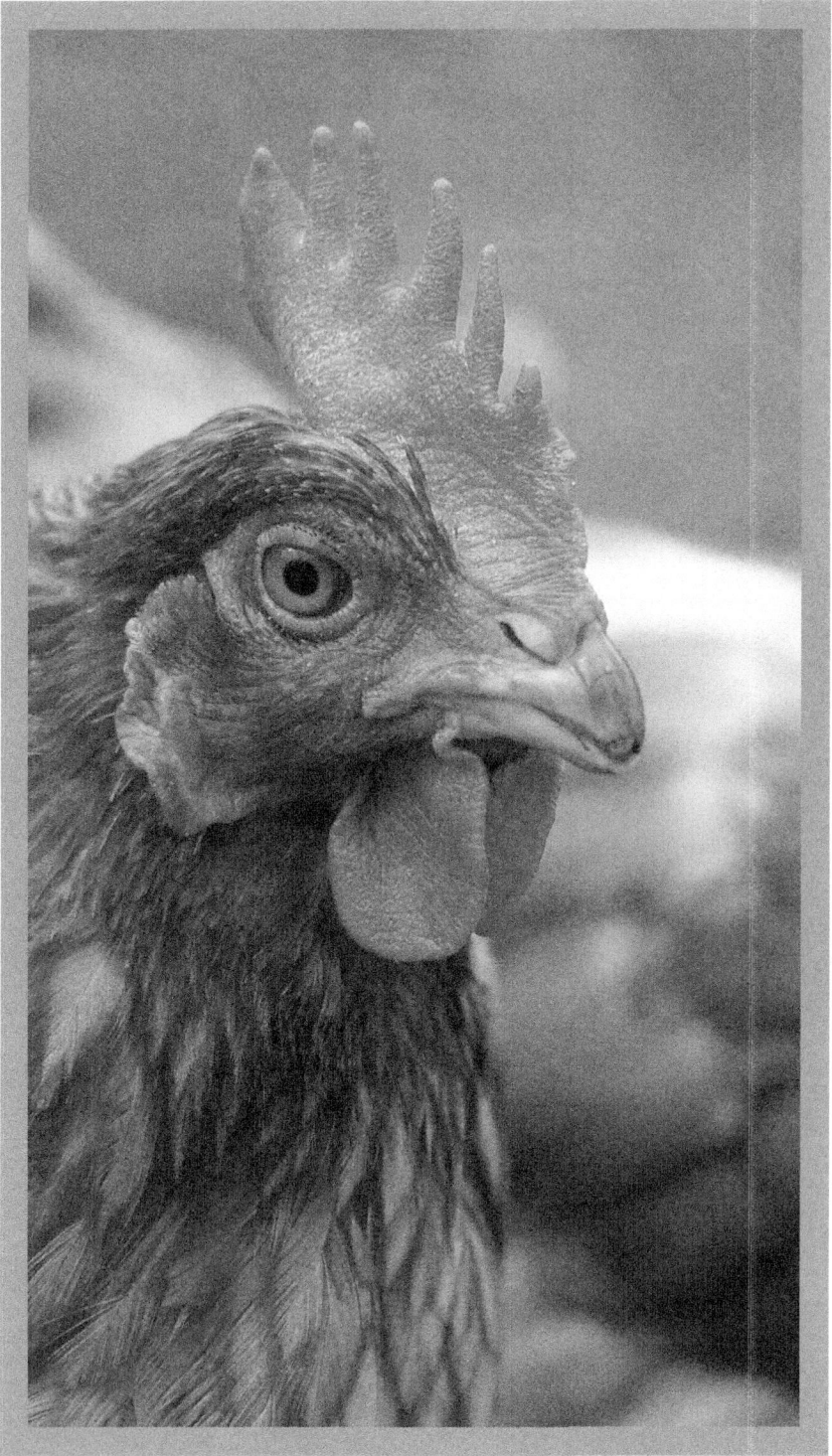

For Jane

❦

Through the growing crack in the delicate shell

A newborn's beak is seen

Then a damp and fragile body

Golden feathers to groom and preen.

A tiny little blue-eyed girl

One of 50,000 others

All born without a nest of straw

All chirping for their mothers.

As days go by her body swells

Her legs begin to ache

The weight is so unbearable

That sometimes legs will break.

She watches others perish

On the feces covered ground

Not capable of reaching food

They starve without a sound.

After 42 short days of life

Still a baby at that age

She's fiercely yanked up by her feet

And thrown into a cage.

Packed so tightly she cannot move

With miles of road ahead

Will she survive this brutal ride

Or be one of the many dead?

At her final destination

When the highway finally ends

She hears the panicked screams of family

The shrieks of frightened friends.

With a pounding heart she sits and waits

She has no other choice

She can't tell them that her foot is stuck

She doesn't have a voice.

When this little girl with sad blue eyes

Is finally ripped away

From the crate that has become her hell

Her little foot will stay.

Severed from her body

No one hears her cry in pain

But I'm not alone in crying now

For this little girl called "Jane."

In the Name of Tradition

In a smothering sea of white

Gentle beauty is lost

Born and bred to be dinner

Whatever the cost.

Debeaked, detoed, crippled and weak

Disease running rampant

Your future is bleak.

In a huge sunless warehouse

Tens of thousands crammed tight

Kept like a secret

Out of mind, out of sight.

When your body is fattened

And you collapse from the weight

You are grabbed by harsh hands

And sent to your fate.

Hung by your feet

Flapping and scared

Still conscious, confused

If only they cared.

Your neck is then slit

By a mechanized blade

As life drains from your body

You're alone and afraid.

Another beside you

Misses the knife

Still conscious, she's boiled

Slowly ending her life.

Neatly you are packaged

Shipped to every store

Butterball makes money

Spent breeding millions more.

Behind the tidy shrink-wrap

Is a mutilated bird

Who had feelings and emotions

And cries that went unheard.

In the name of "tradition"

Tens of millions will die

Somehow their sad remains

Seem so wrong with pumpkin pie.

A Baby's Story

❦

I am born, just one second old

My wriggly red body first feels the cold

As I fall to the floor, there is no soft landing

And the stench in the air, beyond my understanding

My first moments on earth seem somehow all wrong

Where's mama's nuzzle? What's taking so long?

Finally my mouth finds the liquid I crave

With no sign of a nuzzle, I try to be brave

My tiny frame quivers, from fear and from cold

Until finally sleep saves me, this naïve one-day-old.

When my eyes finally open, and I see this awful place

I will see my mama's misery, the sadness in her face

The reason she can't touch me—rusted bars that enslave

The waste on the floor of this huge sunless cave.

Soon I will feel the suffering that billions have to know

Corporate greed surrounds me, as I begin to grow.

Eyes of a Pig

∽

Deep baby blues

Such vast seas of sorrow

They've never seen mercy

And they won't see tomorrow.

Frantically searching

For a shred of relief

From continual torment

And perpetual grief.

They puncture my heart

And bleed my eyes dry

Almost-human, they haunt me

Asking me why.

Begging for kindness

Some semblance of grace

A sweet, hopeful gaze

On each innocent face.

I offer them water

A stroke on the snout

They silently question

If I'll let them all out.

Their senses are heightened

Each sound, each new smell

Since all of their lives

They've been locked inside hell.

They are promised through tears

As the semi departs

I'll continue the struggle

Changing minds, touching hearts.

Your beautiful blues

Will become a clear voice

Pleading please

Make the compassionate choice.

Vanessa Sarges

Bacon

A slab of flesh so grotesquely desired

Drowning in grease, not advised or required

Clogging the arteries, clearly a vice

But the non-human victim pays the real price.

Without anesthesia, as babies they're maimed

Billions of beings, unique but unnamed

Bodies imprisoned, minds that go mad

Severely they suffer, so intensively sad.

Like 3-year old humans, alert and aware

Of stifling indifference so thick in the air

Their only release, a torturous end

They'll never know freedom or the warmth of a friend.

Throats will be slit, blood will be spattered

Consciously boiled, but what does it matter?

Who mourns the loss of each innocent soul?

When misery makes such a great bacon bowl!

Who cares that you pay to put others through hell?

Sizzling sorrow has such a nice smell!

So what if each piece causes torment and pain

There are lives to be lost and diseases to gain!

Each slice of bacon costs more than you think

It belonged to a playful little bundle of pink

With a curious demeanor and a sweet, squishy snout

They're the who, not the what, this poem's really about.

Mother's Day

Gradually her belly swells

Inside he kicks and shifts

Very soon she'll gaze with love

At one of life's great gifts.

Her body labors overtime

Creating and preparing

Nourishment is borrowed through

The bond that they are sharing.

Two harmonizing heartbeats

Separate yet connected

She cradles him internally

So peacefully protected.

When the pushing and the pain subside

She stares into his eyes

Emotion overwhelms her

When she finally hears his cries.

This tiny little being

An extension of his mother

Affection so intense

She's never felt it with another.

Instinctively she guides his mouth

To the fluid he desires

Formulated flawlessly

Nutrition he requires.

Their happiness is fleeting

Their time together, finished

Her milk was never meant for him

It's not to be diminished.

She's helpless to defend him

Despairingly she mourns

Her son was marked for murder

The moment he was born.

A shattered mother, an orphaned son

An excessive price to pay

In an industry where there's no such thing as

Happy Mother's Day.

Tears for my Sisters

❧

I shed tears for my sisters while their rapists are paid

Trained to impregnate and steal babies away.

Violated beauty, bodies abused

Regarded as only machines to be used.

I shed tears for my sisters who become more insane

Through a perverted existence and their captors' disdain.

Ruthlessly exploited, spirits defeated

Assembly-line-style, their torment repeated.

I shed tears for my sisters so mistreated by men

The devoted mother cow, the harmless little hen.

The intelligent sow confined to her crate

Industry dictates that this is her fate.

I shed tears for my sisters as my daughter grows older

And I'm able to kiss her, I'm able to hold her.

She was able to suckle, never stolen away

I was able to watch her get stronger each day.

I shed tears for my sisters because I am free

As a female I question, why them and not me?

Our organs are equal, our purpose the same

Our differences subtle, if only in name.

I shed tears for my sisters whose tears fall as well

With a desperate desire to end this cruel hell.

I can't save their babies, stop their pain or their sorrow

But with my daughter I'll fight for a better tomorrow.

Number 6

❦

The smell of searing flesh and fur

Combined with frantic cries

Imprinted with the number "6"

As tears flow from your eyes.

Numbers don't have pounding hearts

Numbers can't think or feel

A number's pain does not exist

A number's screams aren't real.

Now that you are number 6

Your body will be maimed

Then you'll be sent to slaughter

Conveniently unnamed.

Now that you are number 6

Your suffering diminished

You could just be forgotten

This poem could just be finished.

But you are so much more

Than the brand that stains your hide

A victim of a holocaust

With gentle chocolate eyes.

A unique and tender being

Who should have had a name

No other can replace you

No spirit is the same.

To me you're not a number

Your soul deserves release

With love I call you Calum

Which means purity and peace.

The Plea

Near an overturned trailer, wheels still in motion

Feathers surf wind like the waves of an ocean

Dipping and dancing a soft pirouette

Gracefully pleading, "Please don't forget."

Don't overlook the lives that were lost

Don't undervalue what apathy cost

Don't close your hearts to the pain we endured

To our dismal existence, the cries no one heard.

Wheels now at rest, the cleanup crew arrives

No one speaks about beings, no one talks about lives

How much money was spent? How much money was lost?

Can the truck be repaired? How much will it cost?

"No one was injured," the reporters all say

Just a huge "inconvenience" to commuters today

Not one single mention, no compassionate words

Are spoken in honor of 200 birds.

Bodies casually scraped off the road where they lay

Treated like garbage and thrown away

The cleanup now done, there is almost no trace

But the wind wants an encore and picks up the pace.

White plumage performs one last pirouette

As if to implore, "Please never forget."

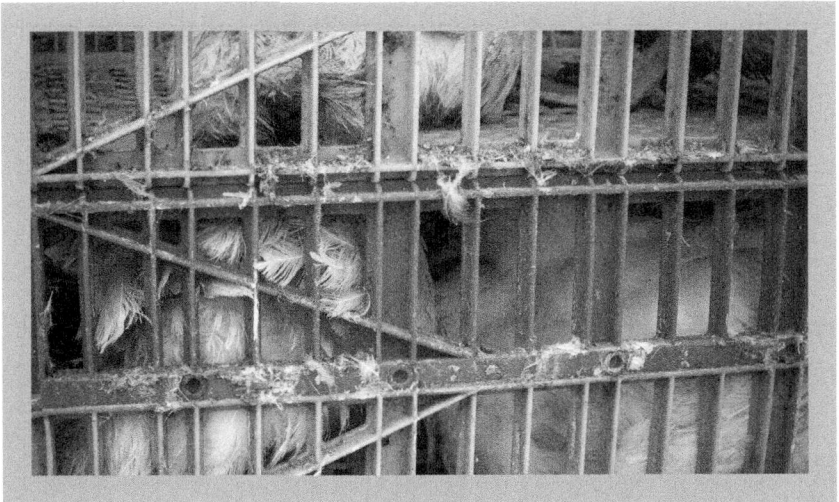

Glass Walls

If walls became huge windows, and we could look inside

When necks were slit and blood was spilled

—If truth could never hide

If what went on behind closed doors was brought into the light

Would our eyelids just close tighter?

Or would we finally do what's right?

If we could watch those innocents fighting their demise

Would tears flow freely down our cheeks?

Would reality trump lies?

If we were forced to witness prolonged suffering and pain

Would indifference fade to empathy—crazy into sane?

If we could finally see a world many knew was there

Would we change the way we live our lives?

Would we then begin to care?

Imagine if we saw ourselves in each and every being

Imagine if there were no walls to block our hearts from seeing.

Would humanity become humane if secrets were revealed?

Would compassion lead our choices when we sat down for a meal?

Or would we adhere to apathy—ignore their anguished cries

As our sisters and our brothers weep and our mother slowly dies.

Modern Slaughter

Behind thick doors

Windowless walls

Dangling bodies bleed.

Despite desperate cries

Frantic fights

Eyes that beg and plead.

Each precious neck

Mutilated

Parting heart from head.

Each sweet brown face

Swiftly stained

A sticky, sickly red.

Life slowly seeps

From each guiltless soul

And falls at the killer's feet.

The butchers continue

On still-conscious minds

Turning muscle into "meat."

Severed vocal chords

Are unsuccessful

Translating pain to sound.

So silently

They suffer

As limbs drop to the ground.

As they hang dying

Piece by piece

This could be called "alarming."

Instead this vile hell on earth

Is simply

"Modern farming."

Dreams

⸎

Vandalized like property
Spray-paint down her spine
Her back defaced with letters
The color of red wine.

Regarded as an object
Like an old, discarded toy
Seven letters seal her fate
Those letters spell DESTROY.

What evil thing must she have done
To be treated with such scorn -
Her murder predetermined
The day that she was born?

Intricately engineered
Manufactured to produce
When her body's been expended
She's no longer any use.

She must have dreamed

Of a better place

Desired to be free

But this tiny metal nightmare

Is all she'll ever see.

She'll only view the outside world

Through slats before her slaughter

Her prison hastily restocked

With someone else's daughter.

I know she dreamed of a better place

I dream now for the others

For sisters, brothers, fathers, sons

For daughters and their mothers.

When this holocaust is history

When compassion conquers greed

Shared dreams become reality

And every soul is freed.

A New Beginning

She gazes with love

Into small almond eyes

And forgets for a moment

The buzzing of flies.

He looks up at her

In an instant he knows

She'll keep him safe

And help him to grow.

Just as their bond

Begins to grow strong

He's pulled away roughly

Something is wrong.

He looks back at her

She gets further away

She lets out a cry

She wants him to stay.

Distress disregarded

Fear forgotten so well

He's forced onto a ramp

On the road to his hell.

Crammed into a truck

With so many others

All of them frightened

Torn from mothers.

When the truck finally stops

They're led out one by one

Chained by the neck

Denied mom's milk and sun.

There in the darkness

In tiny stalls they wait

Unable to move

Unaware of their fate.

Mechanical hands and hormones

Having babies ripped away

Soon take their toll on her

She has just one more day.

As she's shoved into a truck

He's hauled into another

By this same time tomorrow

He will finally see his mother.

But this time will be different

No bars, no crate, no chain

Sunlight replaces darkness

Pastures replace the pain.

The bond they share can grow this time

They'll never have to part

They'll live as nature meant them to

As they should have from the start.

Smile, Tallulah

On a country road you sit alone

Confused by passing cars

Ears notched, tail cropped, someone's property

Yet somehow, here you are.

Born into an industry

that sells you off for parts

You must have seen the darkness

Humans without hearts.

Did you sense your mother's sorrow

Before this fateful day

Did you look into her desperate eyes

As you were ripped away?

Did you see her tiny prison

The boredom she endured

Did depression overwhelm you

With every cry you heard?

You sit outside the shadows now

But what about the others

Where are your suffering sisters

Where are your brutalized brothers?

You're just one among billions

Your life somehow spared

Now you're given a chance

To find humans who care.

A lost little miracle

You have so much to teach

So many minds to change

So many hearts to reach.

You're a special girl, Tallulah

And now you're on your way

To a place you only dreamed about

To live out all your days.

Your worried face grows more relaxed

And with every passing mile

Your pain and fear begin to fade

And I think I see a smile.

Smile, Tallulah, smile.

No Longer a Number

A tender ear punctured, a bright yellow tag

You are now number 151

Just another component of the dairy machine

A cog 'til we say you are done.

You'll generate babies, byproducts to us

We'll take them the day they are born

Industry's indifferent to heartbroken mothers

Money doesn't care if you mourn.

You'll produce what we need to live in our mansions

To pay for our luxury cars

Pain is your prison, you secretly suffer

Your misery safe behind bars.

You barely existed until one fateful day

Kindness freed you and gave you a name

Number 151 is now Lily

And your life is no longer the same.

You are somebody now, not just something

No longer a unit or part

Compassion knew you counted

Time promised to heal your heart.

To you it's just a nightmare now

But for billions more it's real

It's business as usual

Imprison, rape, and steal.

To the 152s and the 251s

To every number without a choice

I'll never stop telling your stories

I'll never stop being your voice.

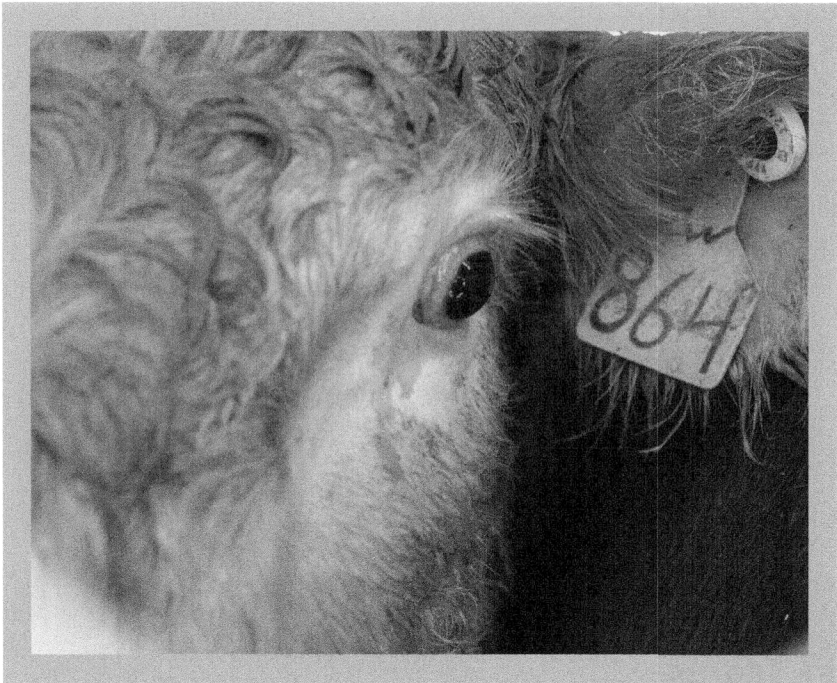

Red Light

At the place where highway 30

Crosses highway 109

I won't forget that summer day

Your frightened eyes met mine.

Through tiny oval openings

In your hell on eighteen wheels

I stared into your guiltless soul

Now I know how terror feels.

Your back was bruised and bleeding

The result of panicked feet

Attached to desperate bodies

Slowly baking in the heat.

How long had you been traveling

Would you make it there alive

Without a drop of water

Just how long could you survive?

I knew where you were going

And that you could sense the sorrow

If you made it through this brutal trip

You'd still not see tomorrow.

Your hopeless eyes engulfed my heart

That August afternoon

For the first time I looked differently

At my fork, my knife and spoon.

I wanted more than anything

To take you from that truck

To quench your thirst and heal your wounds

To somehow change your luck.

I knew those eyes would haunt me

Such despair I'd never seen

So I made you a promise that fateful day

Just before the light turned green.

What if it Were Me

He's just a baby yet he'll never reach one

I could hide behind a smile

They travel without water in the scorching sun

Mile after mile.

She's fattened with babies that she'll never know

I could go about my day

They're denied any food because production is slow

It's the American way.

He cries in the dark for a mother he needs

I could say he isn't real

She's dismembered alive when stunning doesn't succeed

I could say she doesn't feel.

Chains hang heavy from his tender neck

I could say that I don't care

She is desperate to move, they are desperate to peck

I could say that they aren't there.

They are knee-deep in waste and writhe with disease

I could just close my eyes

To oozing sores and broken bones

To greed and corporate lies.

They suffer in silence, their secrets well kept

I could just let it be

Instead I can't stop thinking

What if it were me?

Why Vegan?

Her desperate cries could brand a soul

With agonizing sorrow

When the newborn son she had today

Is stolen from her tomorrow.

This broken heart won't be her last

She'll never be a mother

While misery seeps into milk

That's swallowed by another.

The frantic way he kicks and fights

And tries to cling to life

While men in blood-soaked aprons

Coldly end it with a knife.

How indifferently they slice and dice

What a horrifying fate

When muscle soaks up fear and pain

Ending up on someone's plate.

Despair has overcome her mind

As she takes each labored breath

Feces coat the rusty bars

Inside she waits for death.

For her the torment just won't end

Though many more have died

Each egg absorbs depression

To be broken, flipped and fried.

When suffering is shrink-wrapped

It betrays so many lives

Few realize that they make a choice

With their spoons, their forks, and knives.

When cruelty comes in a carton

And we can package pain

We must see past exteriors

We have so much to gain.

Letter to my Unborn Child

❦

You'll never watch an elephant standing on her head

You will see amazing acrobats and painted clowns instead.

You'll never color Easter eggs or eat a "Happy" Meal

Instead you'll give pigs belly rubs – You'll know chickens

dream and feel.

The clamor from the ice cream truck won't be music to your ears

You will know your Soy Delicious caused no suffering or tears.

You may hear a gentle gobble as you softly stroke a turkey

And give thanks that she's alive as you're eating your Tofurky.

While other kids buy leather shoes and eat at Chuck E. Cheese

You'll be kissing cows and feeding goats and saying "vegan please!"

Being different can be hard I know—this world is often cruel

Maybe you'll be laughed at by the other kids at school.

But compassion is a vital gift that too few share with others

And your heart will not be filled with guilt the way it

plagues your mother's.

So don't ever be embarrassed or ashamed because you care

You'll be uniquely beautiful with an empathy that's rare.

And when you see a rescued lamb and touch his thick warm fleece

You'll feel no sadness or remorse—you can look at him in peace.

What took so long for me to learn, I'll start teaching

you from birth

And your footprint will be much tinier on this fragile earth.

To My Daughter

Look my sweet girl, at her long gentle face

Those tender, trusting eyes

She's a mother like me, with a daughter like you

Please don't listen to the lies.

Her milk isn't meant for humans

It's to make her baby strong

And stealing something that isn't ours

Is always very wrong.

Look my sweet girl, at his cute squishy face

Those deep, engaging eyes

He has a name, just like you and me

Please don't listen to the lies.

He's not another breakfast food

To go with toast and fruit

He loves his life, fresh air and mud

Let's watch him roll and root.

Look my sweet girl, at her delicate face

Those tiny, inquisitive eyes

She's pleasant and curious, and like you, she has friends

Please don't listen to the lies.

She's not another egg machine

To be crammed into a cage

Let's let her dust-bathe in the sun

And live to a ripe-old age.

Look my sweet girl, at the beauty and grace

The affection that animals give

Without them the world's a much gloomier place

So together we'll help more to live.

My Daughter's Eyes

❧

Irreplaceable souls, each structure unique

Warmly wrapped in skins

Innumerable hues, some ornately adorned

In feathers, fur or fins.

Each one is a gift, a potential new friend

Accepted with affection

Two legs or four, in any shade

Not one will face rejection.

Diversity in packaging

Stimulates the heart

It expands as it appreciates

Each stunning work of art.

Gazing through her lenses

Like a child, not a mother

The world is full of brilliance

None more precious than another.

A vibrant collage of colors

Each sculpture has a place

Each painting is a masterpiece

Each species, gender, race.

If everyone could focus

With eyes of just eight years

Prejudice would fade away

Evaporating fears.

In a mind that's not yet molded

Conditioned to condemn

No distinction is created

Disconnecting "us" from "them."

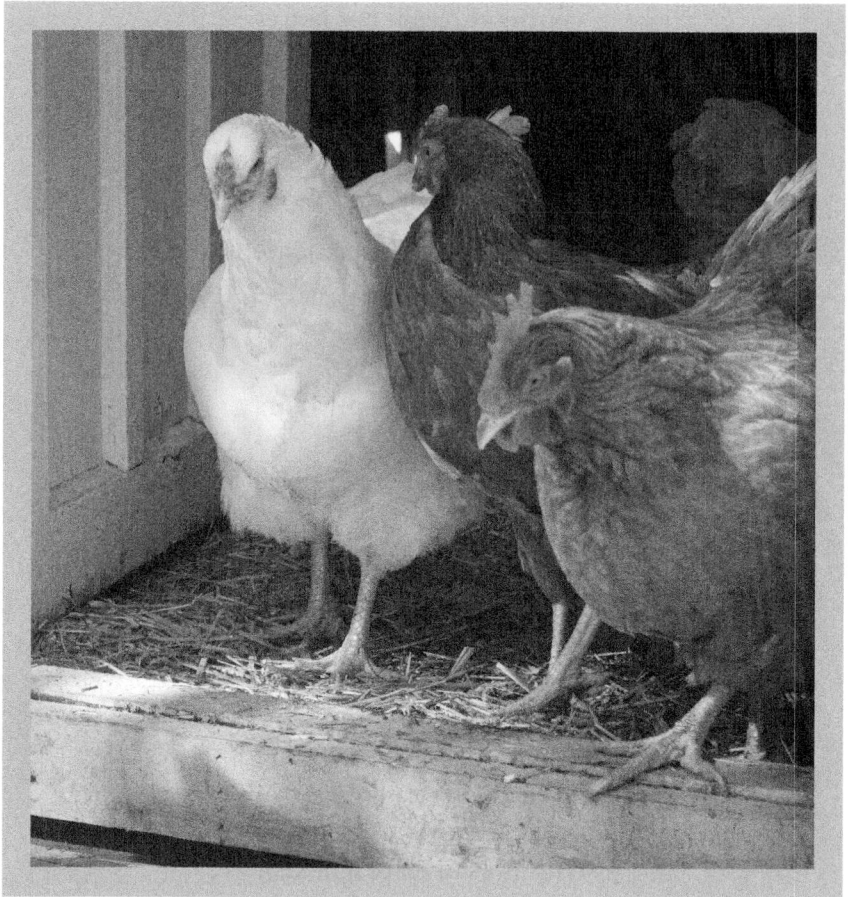

Before innocence is poisoned

With intolerance and lies

There is infinite potential

Through my daughter's eyes.

If Your Tears Were Human

Your language, to us, is foreign

Yet your fear is still the same-

We don't always notice tears fall

But your body feels the pain.

Your happiness is stolen

Like hope once in your eyes-

So many like you suffer,

So much beauty dies.

Your body is our catalyst

To supply what we demand

A Burger joint, a vast buffet

The corner hot dog stand

Your cries fall onto callous ears

Your voice goes unheard

As vocal chords cannot convey

A single human word.

If your tears were human

And you could speak with words-

Your suffering might touch more hearts

Your pleas just might be heard.

If only you could paint your pain

Write a melancholy song-

Maybe then we'd understand

Hurting you is wrong.

I hope someday we understand

What we should have all along.

Breaking the Silence

❦

Silence ensures that the meek are restrained

The harmless held captive, the innocent chained

A menacing friend to corruption and greed

Through deafening silence no soul will be freed.

Silence aids slaughter and vicious assault

The world is a witness, yet no one's at fault

An ally to those who exploit for gain

Whose power is seized through oppression and pain.

One caring expression can shatter the silence

Like a stone through a window, revealing the violence

If one tiny seed can alter our choices

We could cultivate peace with an army of voices.

When silence is broken and compassion is heard

Tyranny fails and becomes just a word

When our hearts are exposed and we let ourselves mourn

Mercy trumps malice and empathy's born.

When justice prevails and all life is protected

Only then will we see we are closely connected

When egos are small and no longer shortsighted

Only then will we realize we are earthlings united.

Compassionate Links

chooseveg.com

cok.net

earthlings.com

farmsanctuary.org

forksoverknives.com

julieoneill.com

mercyforanimals.org

onestepforanimals.weebly.com

ourhenhouse.org

sashafarm.org

thegentlechef.com

torontopigsave.org

vegankit.com

veganoutreach.org

vegweb.com

weanimals.org

wishingwellsanctuary.org

"But for the sake of some little mouthful of flesh we deprive a soul of the sun and light, and that proportion of life and time it had been born into the world to enjoy."

—PLUTARCH

About the Author

Heather Leughmyer graduated from Indiana-Purdue University with a B.A. in English Writing and Linguistics. She is a dedicated vegan, animal rights activist and animal rescuer.

Writing has been a passion of hers for as long as she has advocated for animals. By telling their stories and illustrating their pain she hopes to touch a few hearts and change a few minds with her words.

Heather is the author of *If Your Tears Were Human, Adopting Adele, Brave Benny, Courageous Conner, Dandelion's Dream, Elyse's Escape,* and co-editor of *Rescue Smiles.* She lives in Columbia City, Indiana, with her husband, daughter and several animal companions.

About the Photographer

❦

Vanessa Sarges wanted to make more of a contribution to Animal Rights, and felt that there was no better way to do so than to document their lives through her photography.

She began bearing witness with Toronto Pig Save and capturing the souls who were being transported to slaughter and the brave activists bearing witness with her. Although taking those photos is both sad and infuriating, many people have contacted Vanessa to say that her photos were the turning point of their lives and that they were transitioning to a vegan lifestyle as a result.

Vanessa and Heather have been friends for many years and Vanessa has taken great inspiration from their friendship and from Heather's profound poetry. Vanessa was honoured to be asked to contribute to *If Your Tears were Human*.

We hope you'll give If Your Tears Were Human *a review on Amazon and other venues. Your reviews mean the world to our authors, and help books such as this one reach a wider audience. Thank you so much!*

About Who Chains You Books

PUBLISHING FOR ANIMAL LOVERS, ACTIVISTS, AND RESCUERS.

Love Animals? Welcome! Our books applaud animals and those who care for them, and we celebrate the connection between humans and our non-human friends. At Who Chains You we publish books for those who believe people—and animals—deserve to be free.

Our mission is singular: to amplify the voices of the animals through the empowerment of animal lovers, activists, and rescuers to write and publish books elevating the status of animals in society.

Who Chains You Publishing brings you books that educate, entertain, and share gripping plights of the animals we serve and those who rescue and stand in their stead.

Read more about us at whochainsyou.com.

Printed in Great Britain
by Amazon

21276894R00051